I0429318

Brian Rider

Mini Guide
2 Point Perspective

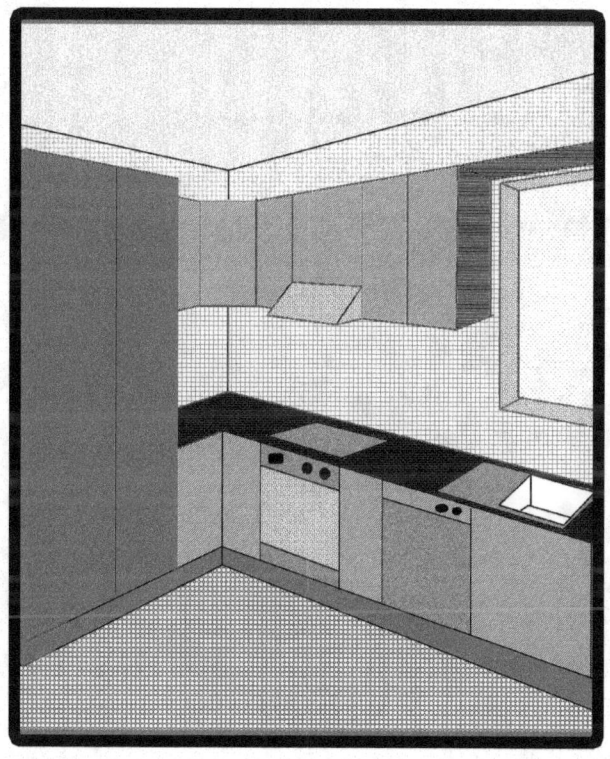

Mini Guides 2016

Foreword

Thank you for choosing one of our New
Mini Guides. The purpose of these guides
is to provide a simple compact training
guide in a variety of KBB and Interior
Designer or even Exterior Designer titles
which extract the highly focussed
information from our giant tomes that ran
about 1000 pages and which would cost a
lot more than you would wish to pay or we
would wish to charge, With our mini
guides you can acquire any of the titles at
an extremely modes targeted sum.

1

COPYRIGHT

©century 21 publishing 2016

Please note all material contained within this publication is
the property and copyright© of the publishers Century 21
and the Author Brian Rider. All rights are reserved

2

The Vanishing Point

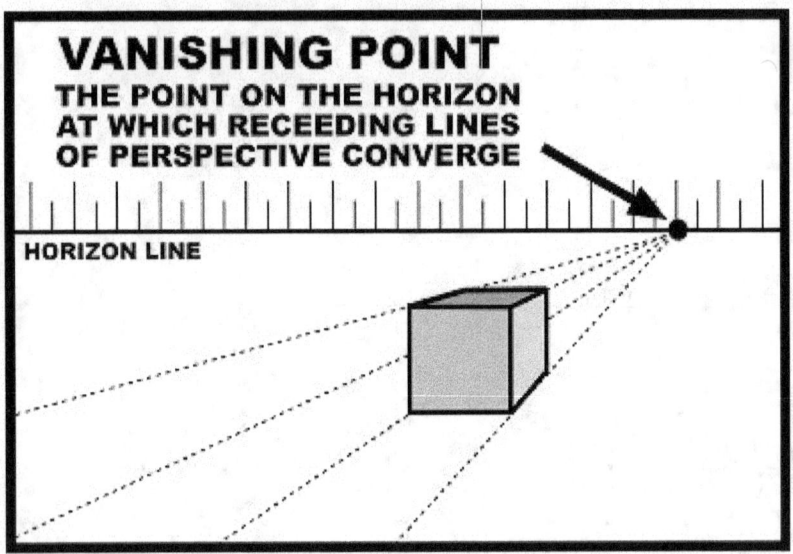

VANISHING POINT
THE POINT ON THE HORIZON
AT WHICH RECEEDING LINES
OF PERSPECTIVE CONVERGE

HORIZON LINE

THE VANISHING POINT

Isometric & axonometric drawings use parallel lines so do not need a vanishing point

Perspective drawings use vanishing points. However return measurements may require the positioning of another VP although we tend to call this the viewing point.

The positioning of the VP is critical in having the best view of the subject. In KBB projects we recommend eye height. You then get the same view as you wish to sell to the customer The method is less formal and less accurate than the Axonometric and Isometric drawings but far more artistic and flexible..

As before start with a scale plan. If you haven't got one, make one using the example as a guide

Vanishing point was found, in the 14th century. I am skeptical. The vanishing point is obvious in drawings & real life. Look at the railway perspective. . There weren't any prehistoric railways but many instances would have indicated the use of a vanishing point. Remember-Neanderthal man left some quite elaborate drawings in their dwelling caves??

The 1 point method is quite straightforward. All lines on the back wall of height and width are completely square and in scale. All lines projecting from the back wall into the depth of the drawing are perspective lines drawn from the vanishing point. 2 point is quite different and you will see this method in a separate guide

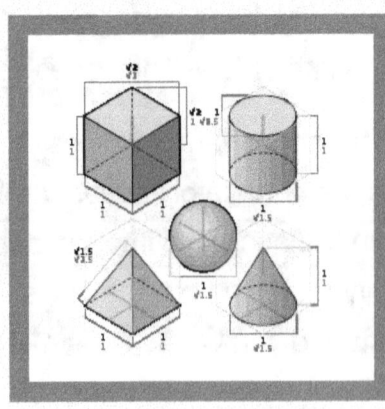

Remember for odd shapes always start with a box and then create the shape within the box

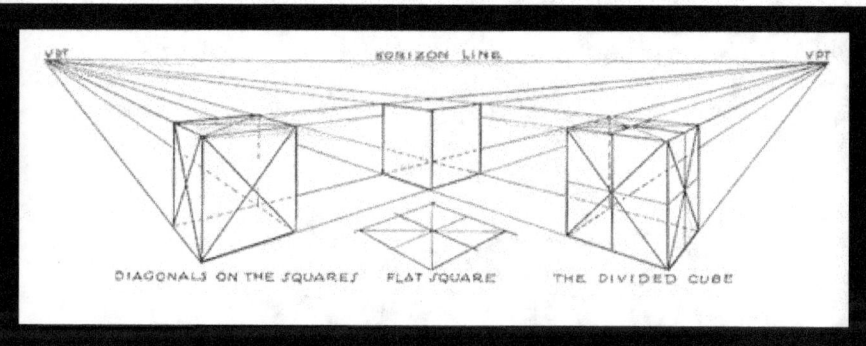

DIAGONALS ON THE SQUARES   FLAT SQUARE   THE DIVIDED CUBE

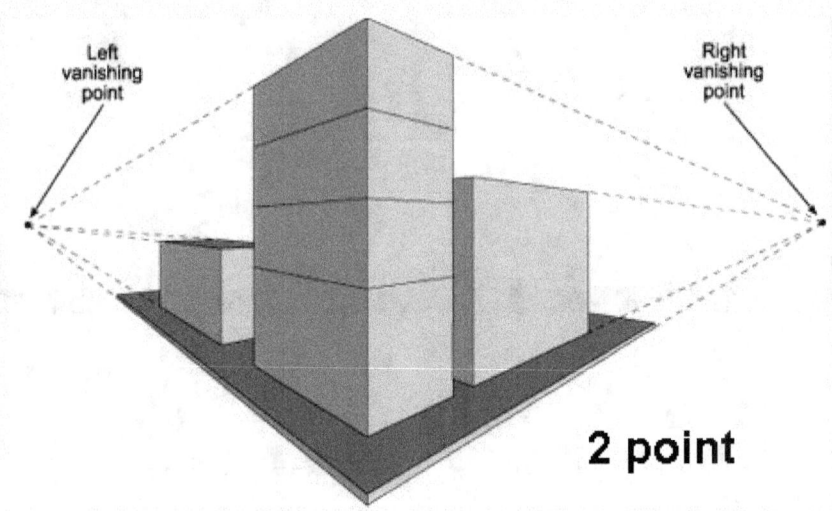

Left vanishing point

Right vanishing point

2 point

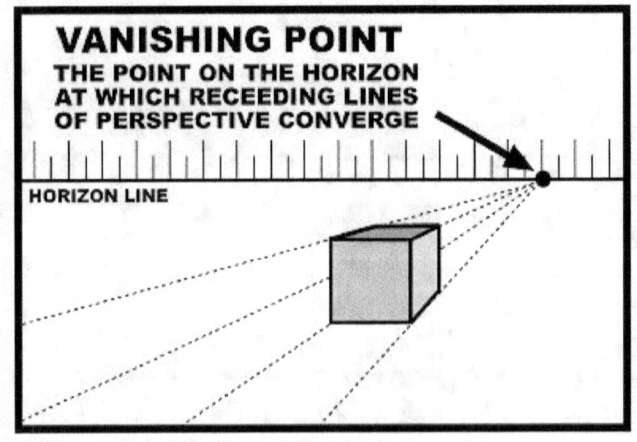

VANISHING POINT
THE POINT ON THE HORIZON
AT WHICH RECEEDING LINES
OF PERSPECTIVE CONVERGE

HORIZON LINE

2 Point Guidelines.

There are certain aspects with 2 point drawing which makes it more complex than 1 point. Only the back corner wall as in an L shape kitchen is in scale and square. As you move into the drawing the front face of everything is also square but not in scale but because it is square you can project lines and determine the location with the measurement techniques and then finish the profile - such as the end of a carcase line simply using your parallel and set square of your drawing board. If you are using a computer drawing system you select the shift key or similar to force the line to be square both horizontal and vertical. This makes a superb short cut.

Once you have become accustomed to the technique you will also be able to determine measurements either by guestimating or perhaps select a few vital points maybe in 1 metre sections and then insert intermediate locations.

3
Return Wall
Measurements

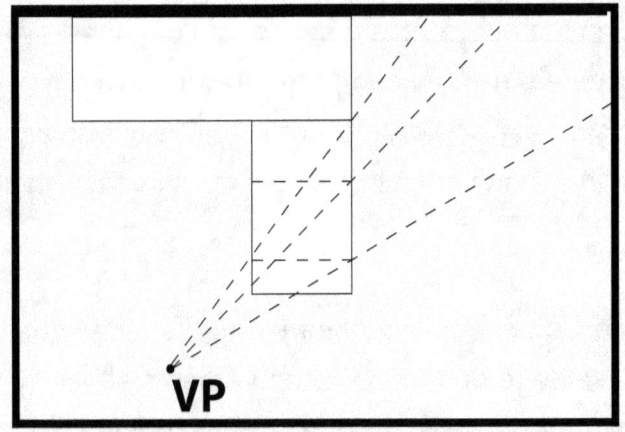

The Formal Method

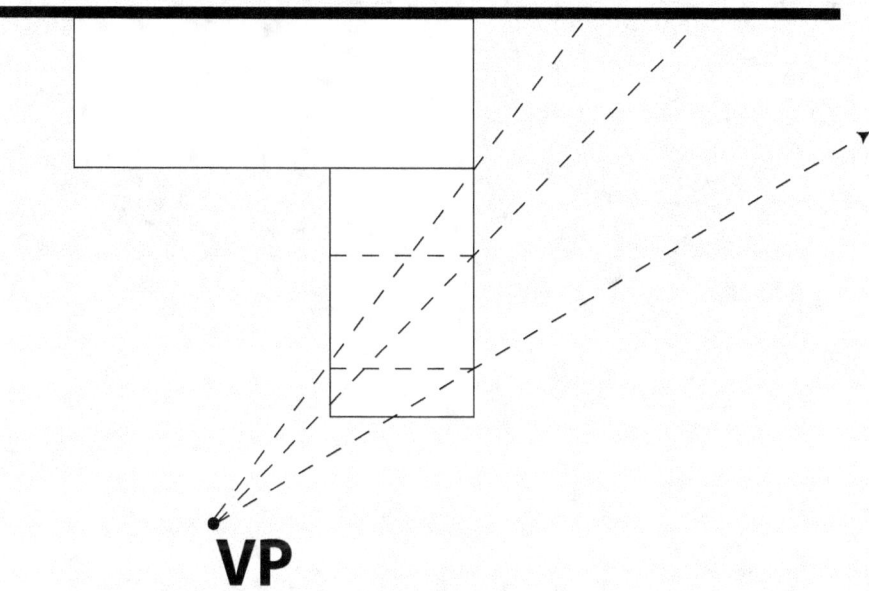

VP

This is the proper method to achieve accurate and consistent return measurements. Please note the VP shown is in fact the viewing point although it is in effect, an additional vanishing point. If you start with your original scale plan you should then transfer the return wall measurements to your perspective drawing (here shown as a group of kitchen units. Choose your VP - it is not critical except the view that it provides. The VP should be as far away as possible on your drawing board or even off the board. Using the VP just like a vanishing point you line up the VP with the measurements of the individual units and project them to the wall shown as a solid line. For a more compact image you would project the floor line in perspective and then transfer the measurements to the floor line instead of the back wall line - the choice is yours. You then draw in perspective from your measurement points

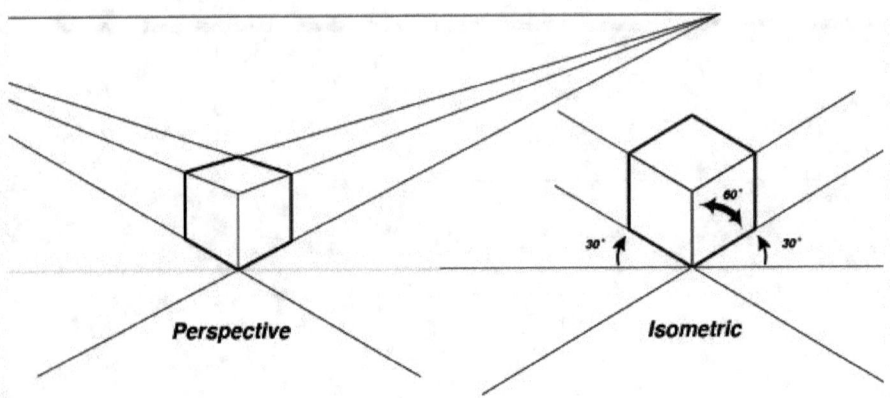

Perspective **Isometric**

The measurement systems are many and various with the perspective ruler being the simplest.

In some respects this is the most difficult aspect of perspective, but mainly 1 point and 2 point perspectives. The method is more or less the same for both so we shall just elaborate on the basic principles.

One of the things that our Designers found was that they could not teach their delegates how to judge the dimensions. We had developed the scale ruler as image. This was simple, effective and allowed the delegates to relax and get on with the more important drawing skills. In fact, it isn't really necessary but it is a big help in distance learning for speed of the drawing and give you confidence to progress. We shall also outline how to locate the return measurements in other ways.

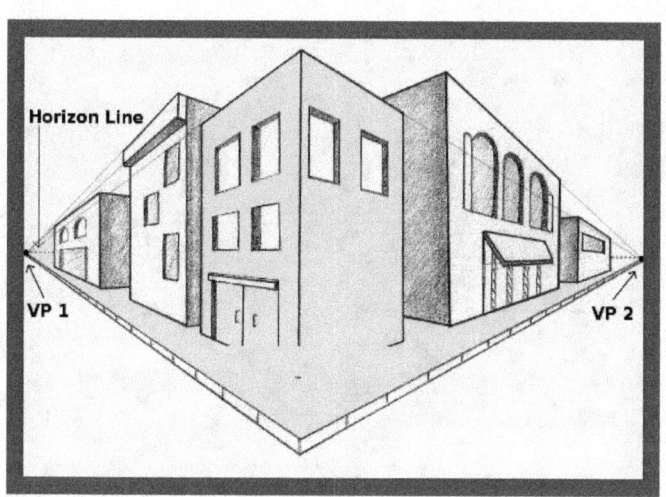

The back corner is simple as this is in scale. The other measurements are perspective measurements so need to be located.

VANISHING POINT & MEASUREMENTS

- think of a railway track
- the perspective goes to 0
- the track separation diminishes
- this is your perspective measurement

12

FINDING THE RETURN MEASUREMENTS

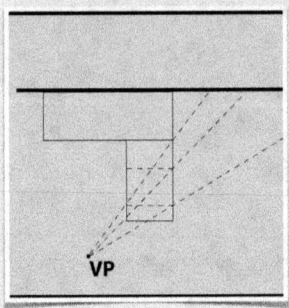

- method 1 using the floor line

METHOD 2

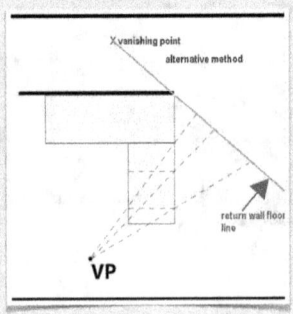

- using the perspective floor measurement

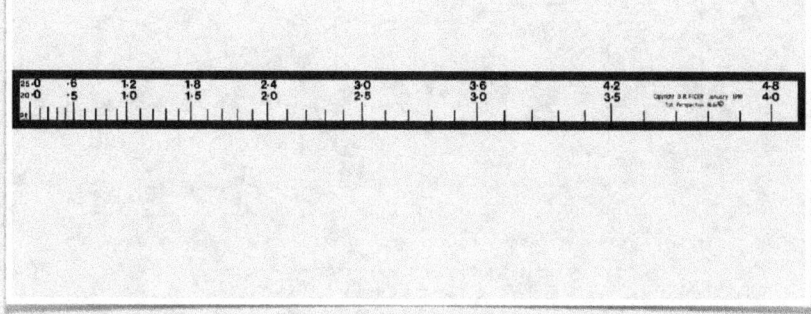

USNG A PERSPECTIVE RULER©

When using a perspective ruler you need to mark the cumulative points. e.g 600mm then 1600mm and perhaps 2200mm etc.

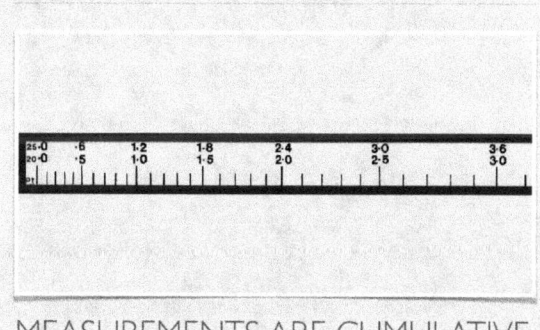

MEASUREMENTS ARE CUMULATIVE

Calculate your measuring points but experience can reduce your reliance

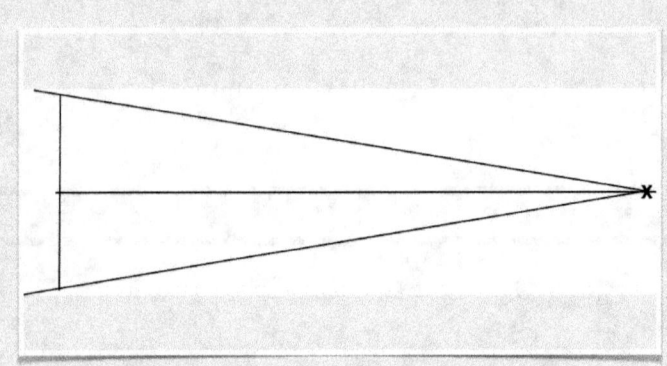

AN ALTERNATIVE METHOD

BUT CAN ALSO USE IN CONJUNCTION WITH THE PERSPECTIVE RULER

INITIAL STEPS-
REFER TO DRAWING 1 PREVIOUS

- locate your vanishing point or use the VP in existing drawing

- draw the horizontal horizon line

- use a convenient measurement above and below the horizon line this line must be equal above & and below HL

- use the end of room or units to produce a vertical line as shown on drawing 1

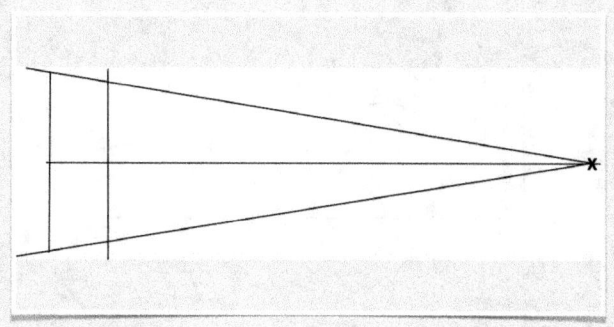

STEP 2

arbitrarily choose your first measurement - we have used 500mm

STEP 3

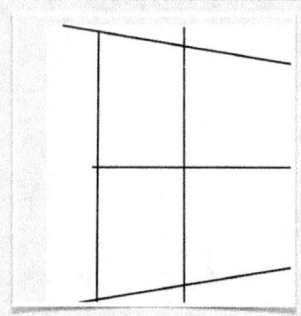

- as you can see, this first measure intersects the HL exactly in the centre of the first division

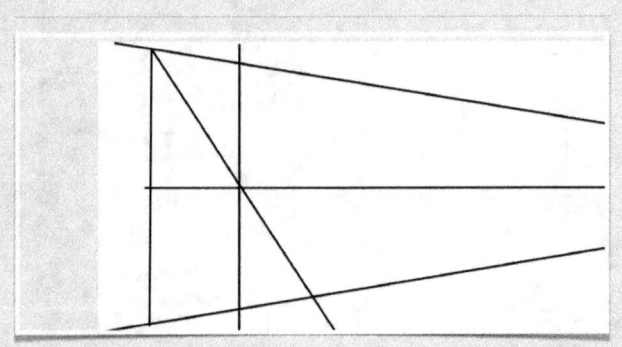

STEP 4

draw a line from the top left of the initial triangle through the intersect of first division

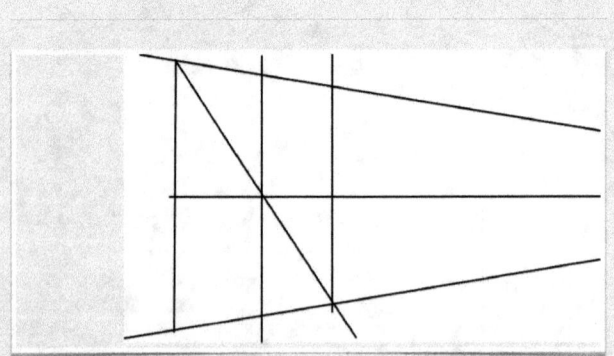

STEP 5

where this line intersects the lower line of the triangle - draw a vertical line - this is division 2 still representing the same size as your initial division i.e in this case 500mm

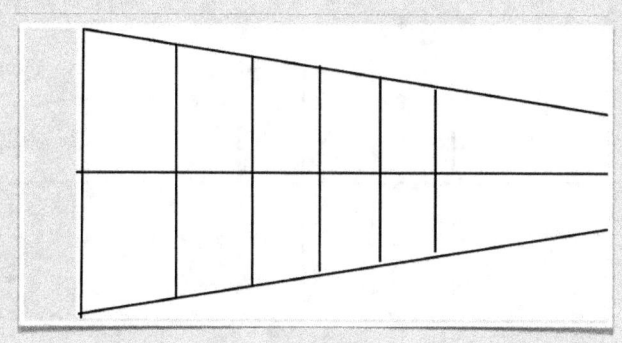

STEP 6

continue producing divisions the using the same method

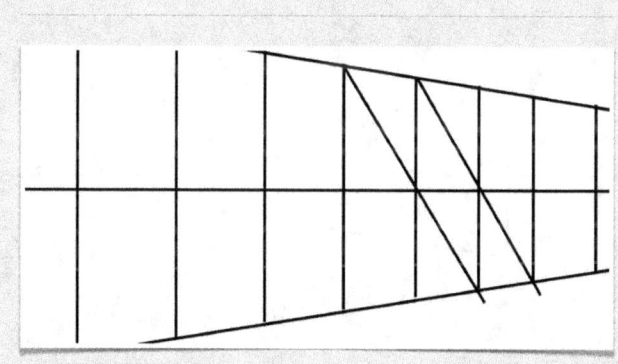

STEP 7

continue with more divisions

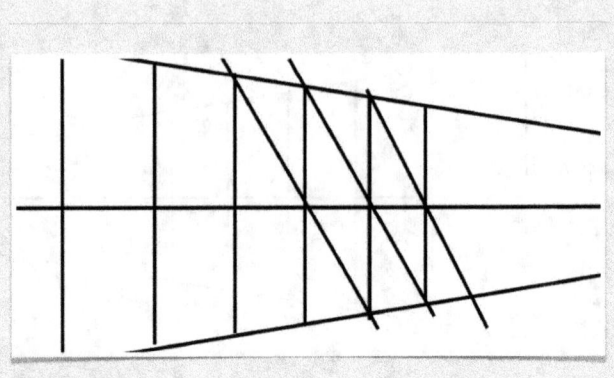

STEP 8

continue with as many divisions as required

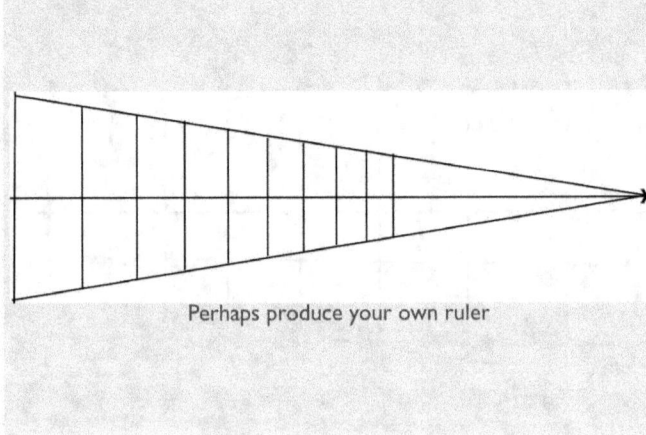

Perhaps produce your own ruler

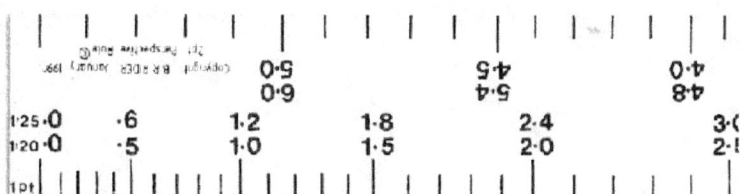

The Perspective Ruler© - as you can see you have a
1 point section and a separate 2 point section each
divided into 1:20 and 1:25 scales.

This is purely for convenience to suit varying sizes of
rooms. The actual measurement depends on your
theoretical viewing position and how much detail
you wish to see on each wall.

This has not been reproduced to the original scale
but as this is interpretive it has no real effect. You
could copy this to a piece of card to use in your initial
drawings.

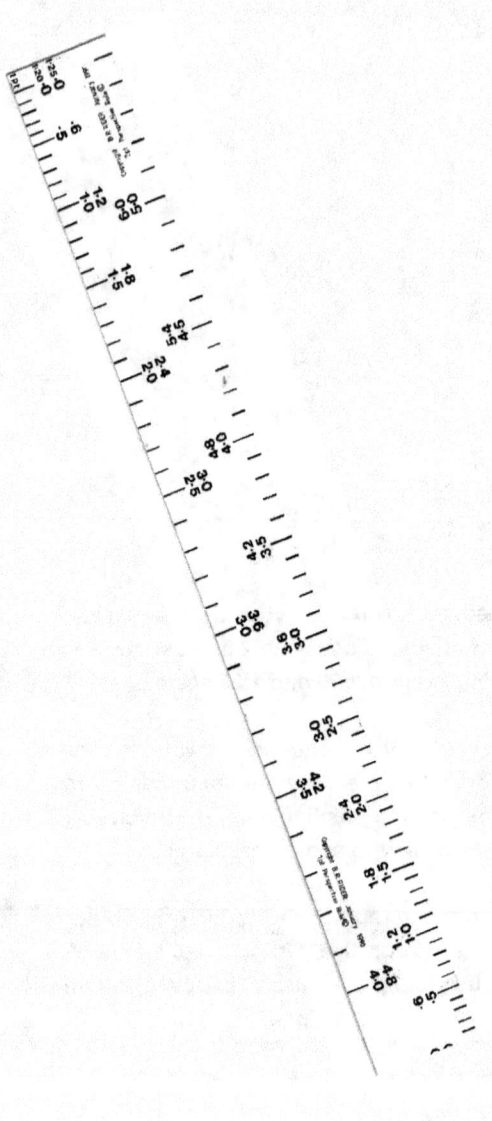

METHOD 2

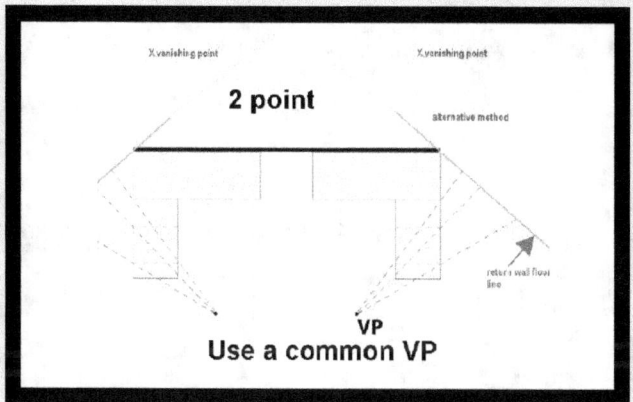

Please note this is the proper layout for 2 point interior drawings

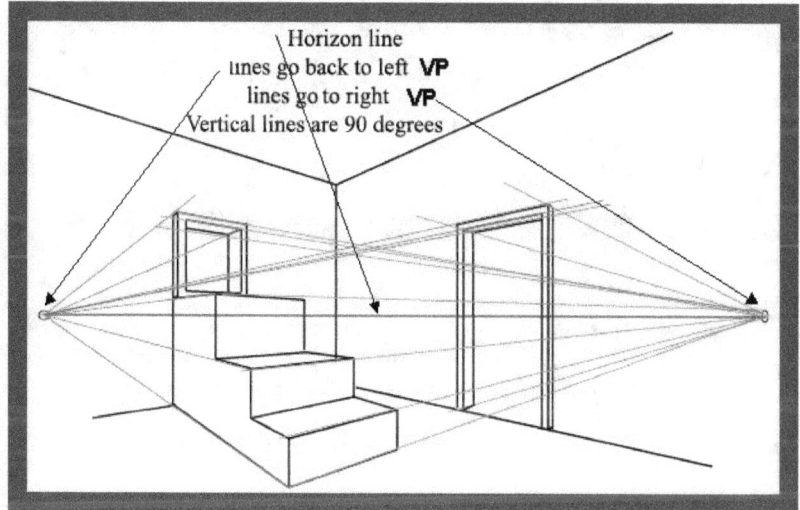

4

2 Point Perspective method

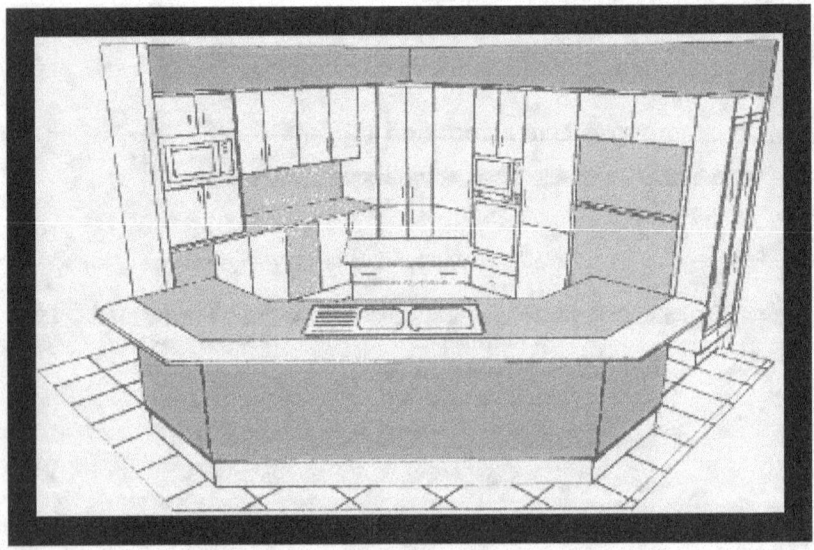

The 2 point is time consuming but generally gives the best view in wide projects such as a large kitchen or bedroom. You can also expand this into a multipoint perspective but probably not necessary.

Start with a Scale Plan

The scale plan is crucial to a any perspective drawing. The problem with 2 point is that only the corner wall starts off in scale and perspective measureents are required for is depth and return walls. Ideal for for L shape rooms.

Step by Step

REMEMBER

1. 2 point is particularly suitable for exterior presentations

2. always remember to use your drawing board

3. all vertical lines should be square

4. all working lines should be from the vanishing points

The 2 Point Perspective drawing is an excellent method for many KBB projects particularly where you have 2 walls you wish to show in detail. We recommend starting with a scale plan to ensure that the 3d can be produced quickly and accurately. It you were drawing a kitchen, you would find the centre wall of the room as in an L shape kitchen and mark off the wall and unit sizes in scale. If you do not know the wall and actual unit sizes you can use the default size of 2m height for tall units or wall units, 900 high for base units, 600 deep for base and tall units and 300 deep for wall units. Wall unit heights can vary but use the set out dimension of 2m and then use an arbitrary 600 or 700 height of wall unit. Standard ceiling height is 2.4m .

 Use light strokes when you draw. Also remember that you will be removing many lines as the drawing progresses so the lighter the better and then you can use a heavier pencil later,

For those of you that have chosen a computer drawing method, you will find that you can select a very faint line to beg in and then remove those lines or replace the lines that are in the way and then change the weight of the line later - in fact it is childishly simple on virtually any drawing programme. To produce an accurate drawing you should also be using a scale ruler but if you do not want to invest in such an item you can use an ordinary ruler and the standard scale of 1:20 i.e. every 1 cm or mm equal 20. You could also use a marking pen to note some of the more commonly used conversion on your cheap wood ruler. i.e. 600mm 1 metre etc.

Once you have produced your basic room outline just pause for a moment to check that have actually produced the right size and shape. Errors at this stage will be compounded at later stages when you start to add detail.

However, I am sure you will want to produce these drawings in the minimum possible time and perhaps spend a little more time on final presentation. If you are using the drawing to sell a project this can be a valuable stage.

As the drawing is takes shape you will find that some of the lines are interfering with your view of the drawing. This is particularly important when you first start drawing as it is more difficult to SEE the actual shapes taking place because of the confusion of the different overlapping lines.

As you progress with the drawing you can remove any lines that will not be required for further detail such as the floor lines which will probably be totally hidden. But remember only to remove the lines or parts of the lines that are not required for the final drawing.

The extent of the detail in the drawing really depends on the project and how much detail would be desirable.

You can add worktop thickness, plinth inset, even the inset of appliance detail but ask yourself "is it worth it?" does the extra time and effort really make that much Saleable detail. Try a few. You will soon be able to use your judgment for that particular project of possibly the client or customer.

When you have reached the end, completion is in the eye of the beholder

It is important to add some rendering but exactly what rendering will depend again on your own judgment of the project and or the client.

This is a colour guide so we are showing mixed rendering. If you are producing copies, monochrome may be your desired answer, especially with the cost of ink if you are using a computer. But , equally, producing a colour rendered drawing is so easy, especially on a computer. Even if you did draw by hand you might even find that scanning your drawing for the final rendering may be the easiest solution but, equally, if you have enjoyed the drawing process which so many people do, you may wish to use your own skills to render the final drawing.

If you are using a computer programme for your drawing method, rendering will be available within the drawing programme or via a separate graphic programme such as Graphic Converter. The variation of colours and patterns is quite remarkable.

It is very easy to get carried away and if this is project you are selling it is well worth getting used to the type of colours and intensity and patterns that your client prefers.

Targeting the drawing specifically for that customer is the easiest way to get them hooked.

2 POINT STEP BY STEP GUIDE

Draw the corner back wall of the room in scale.

Default height is 2400mm

In all cases use the actual dimensions of the units you are drawing if known.

As with all drawings you start with the drawing board and set square   Remember to use portrait or landscape whichever is more appropriate.

Let us assume that the ceiling height is a standard 2.4 metres and the length of the walls are as per your scale plan but need to use a perspective scale for the return measurements.

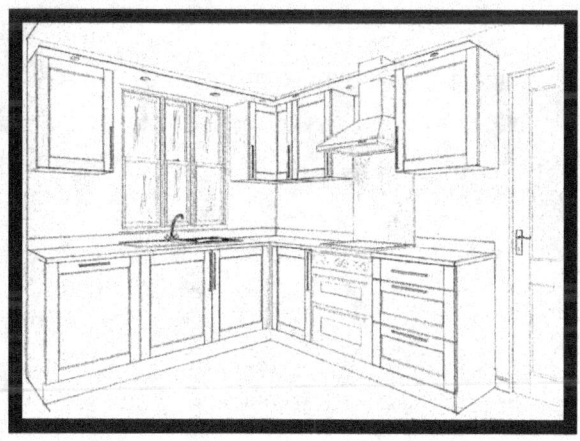

If you wish you can use just a sheet of paper a sturdy ruler and a set square and a scale ruler.

Just make sure that you hold the paper and the rulers and set square steady and use light strokes when you draw. Also remember that you will be removing many lines as the drawing progresses so the lighter the better and then you can use a heavier pencil later,

For those of you that have chosen a computer drawing method, you will find that you can select a very faint line to beg in and then remove those lines or replace the lines that are in the way and then change the weight of the line later - in fact it is childishly simple on virtually any drawing programme.

With your drawing board method many designers like to produce a rough initial drawing and then refine it using tracing paper. You don't even need tracing paper if you purchase some lightweight paper instead. This can actually be quicker. I used to produce copious drawings during a busy period and a colleague would refine the drawings for me. This meant we could product 20-30 full studies a week if necessary.

Most designers tend to use the 1 point for the majority of Interior Design presentations. It is particularly useful when you are presenting a drawing which is predominantly showing one major wall. Where you have a more complex layout you need to use your judgement as to which method to use. Time will tell with experience.

I would also point out the important of the return wall measurements. You will see at the front of this booklet that we invented a perspective ruler, a very simple way of providing return wall measurements. We have, however, shown the alternative methods of producing effective return wall measurements. In all cases however there is an element of judgment. Indeed when we were teaching perspective we actually taught at a Design Academy where the head designer was very proficient at drawing perspectives but she could not teach the delegates how to judge the return measurements. In fact this issue caused more failures on their own perspective courses than any other. When we introduced the perspective ruler, delegates no longer needed to worry about this aspect and were able to get on with the task with relative ease. It is also fair to say that when you first start to draw 3d it is not always easy to see what you are drawing. But, have heart, it will come after practice.

In the early years many designers used to use the grid. Frankly I have always found this more of a distraction than an aid. but it is available if you wish to try. Grids can come with or without the vanishing point but once you establish the basis of the grid you simply trace the grid through. The real negative in using grids is that the drawing is very rigid and inflexible and frankly is extremely boring and hardly artistic.

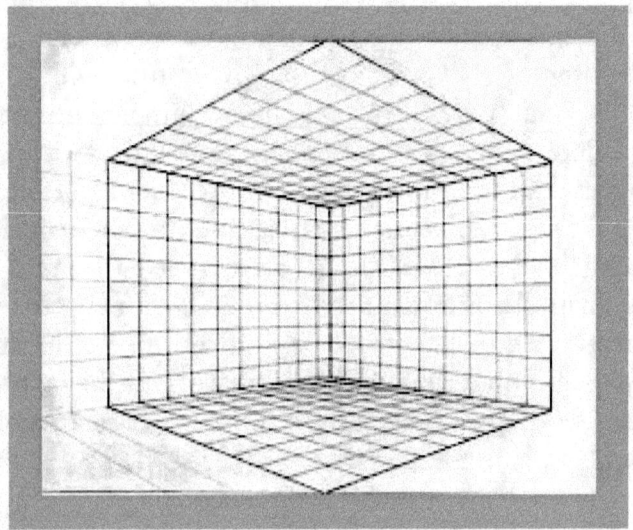

ALWAYS USE A DRAWING BOARD FOR BEST RESULTS

2 POINT STEP BY STEP

STEP 1

PREPARE YOUR SCALE PLAN

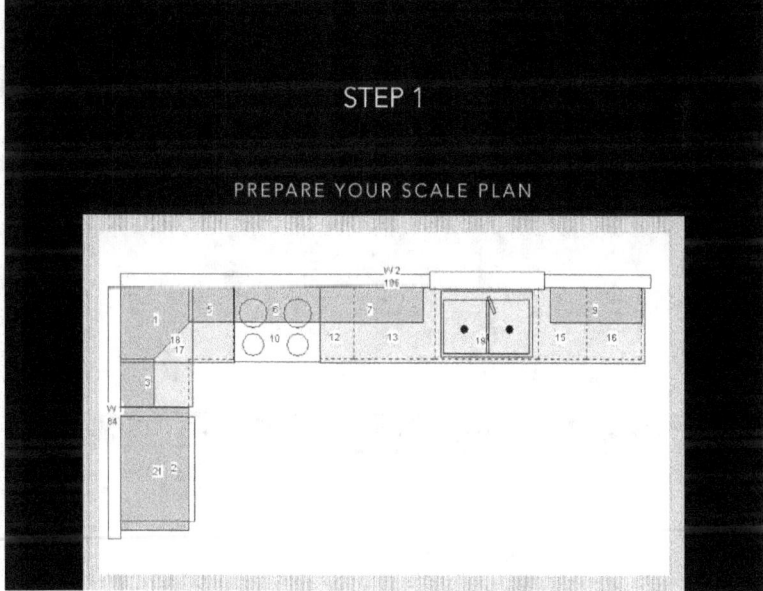

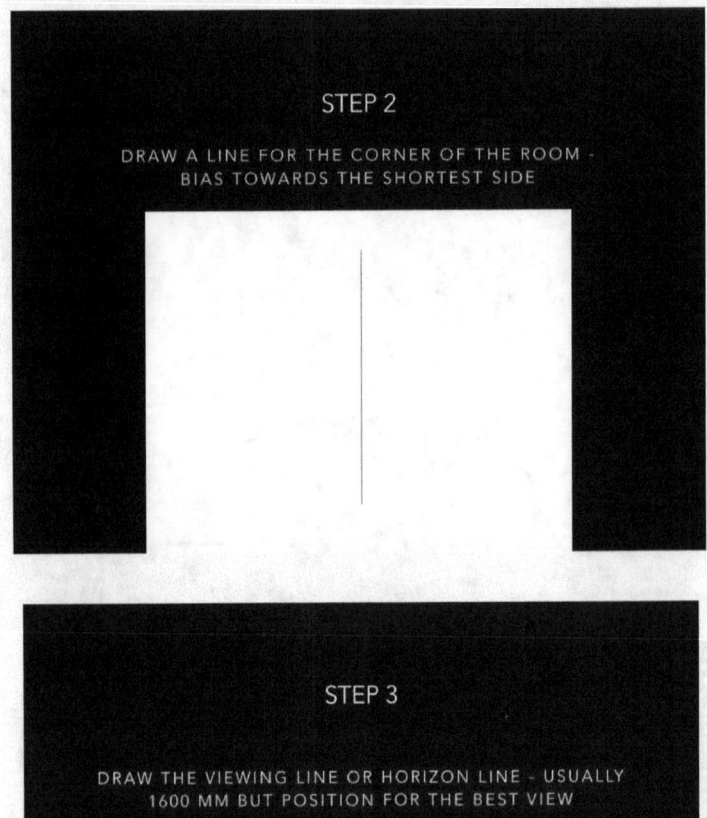

STEP 2

DRAW A LINE FOR THE CORNER OF THE ROOM -
BIAS TOWARDS THE SHORTEST SIDE

STEP 3

DRAW THE VIEWING LINE OR HORIZON LINE - USUALLY
1600 MM BUT POSITION FOR THE BEST VIEW

STEP 4

POSITION YOUR VANISHING POINTS - EASIEST IS ON
THE VIEWING LINE BUT NOT CRITICAL

STEP 4

CLEARLY SHOW HEIGHT OF ROOM - DEFAULT IS 2.4M

Default height is 1600mm

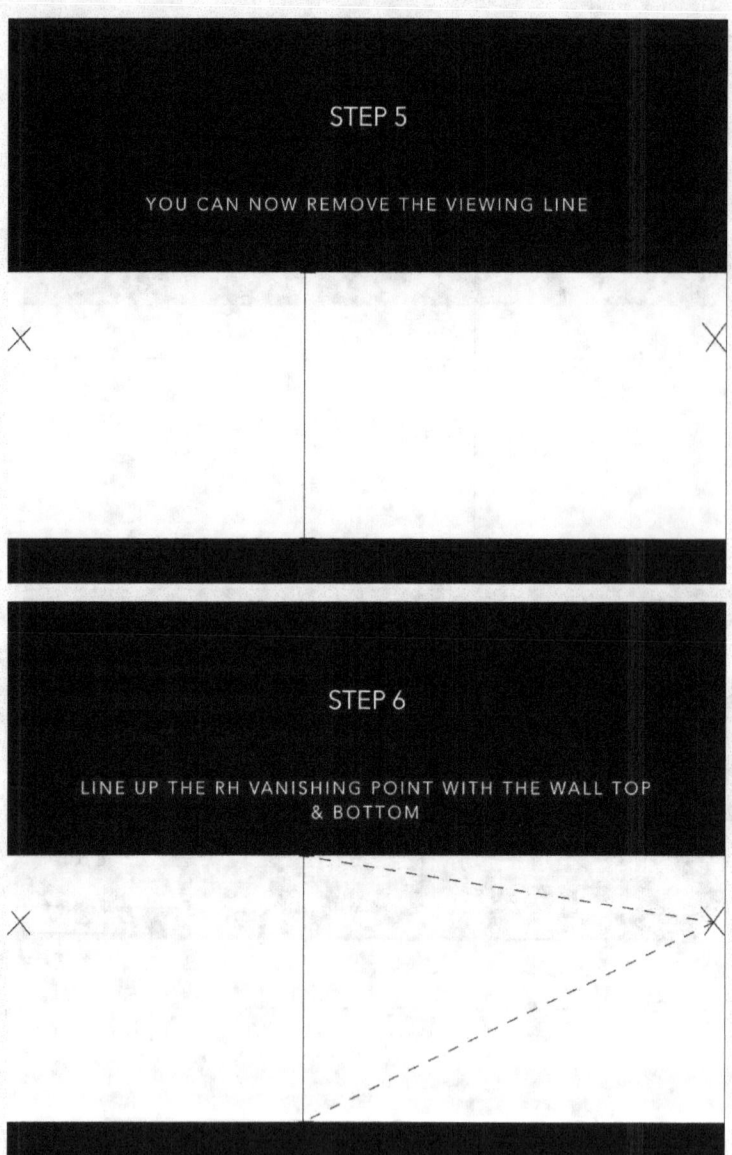

STEP 5

YOU CAN NOW REMOVE THE VIEWING LINE

STEP 6

LINE UP THE RH VANISHING POINT WITH THE WALL TOP
& BOTTOM

STEP 7

DRAW A LINES THROUGH THE WALL MEASUREMENT TO REPRESENT THE LH WALL

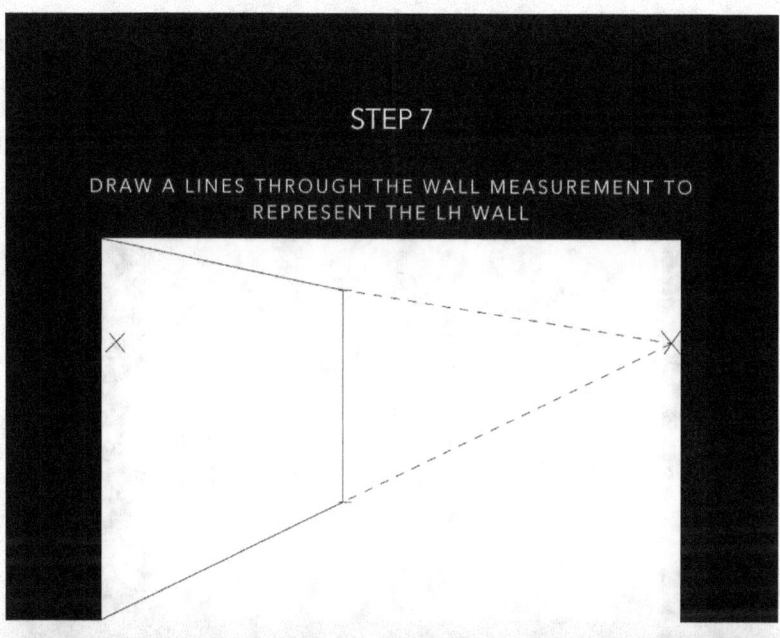

STEP 8

REPEAT FOR THE RH WALL

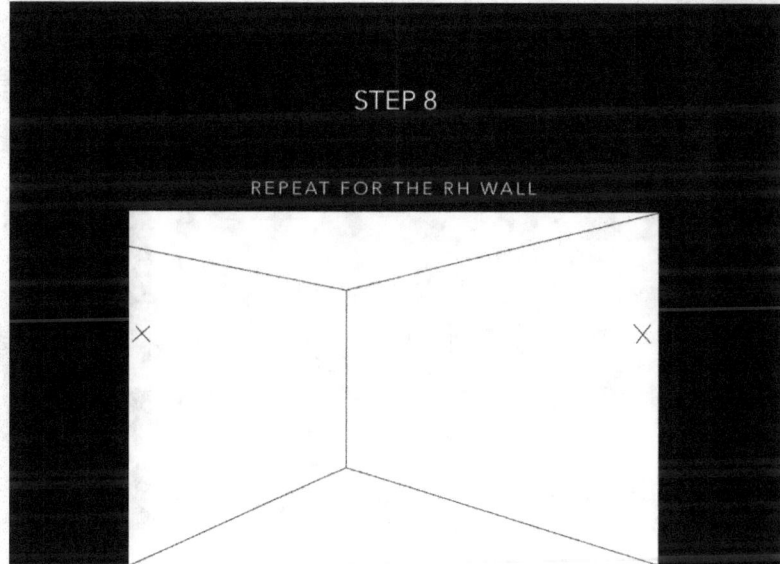

You will need to use the perspective measurement techniques to locate these measurements.

STEP 9

MARK OFF THE WORKTOP HEIGHT AND WALL UNIT TOP

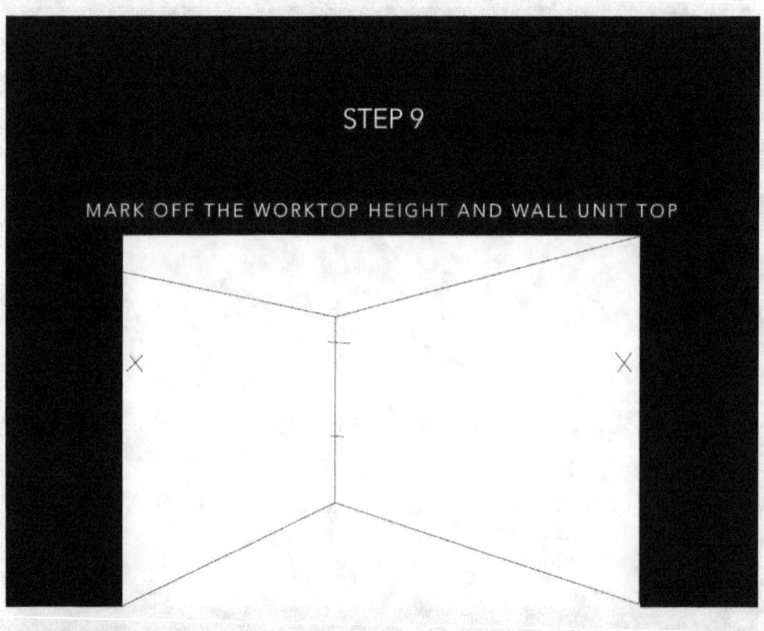

STEP 10

PROJECT THESE LINES ACROSS THE RH WALL

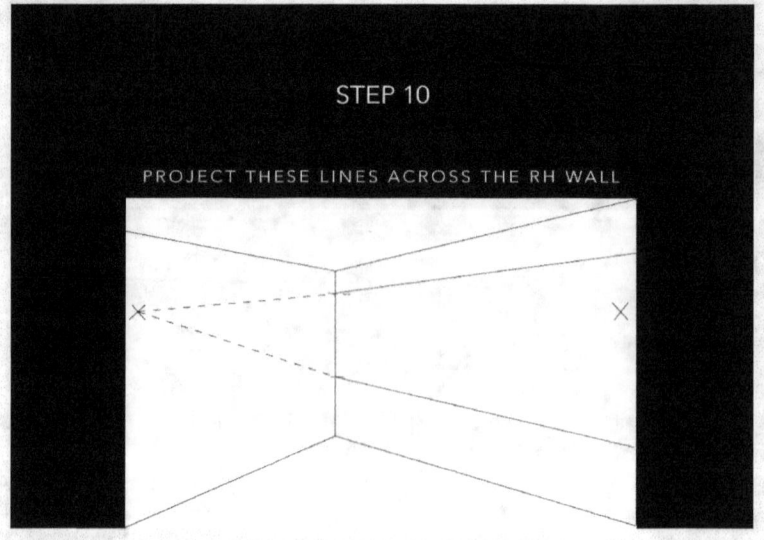

STEP 11

REPEAT FOR LH WALL

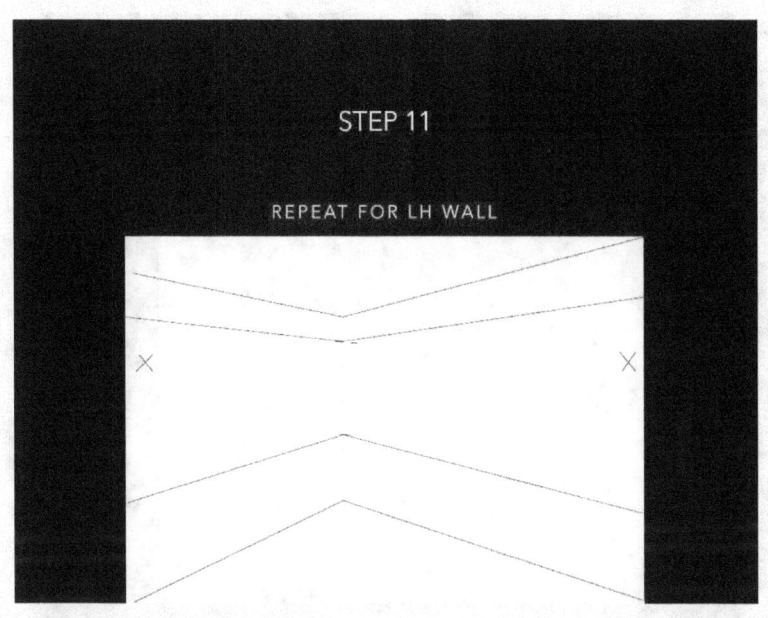

STEP 12

YOU CAN NOW REMOVE THE MEASUREMENTS AND
DIMINISH THE VANISHING POINTS IF YOU WISH

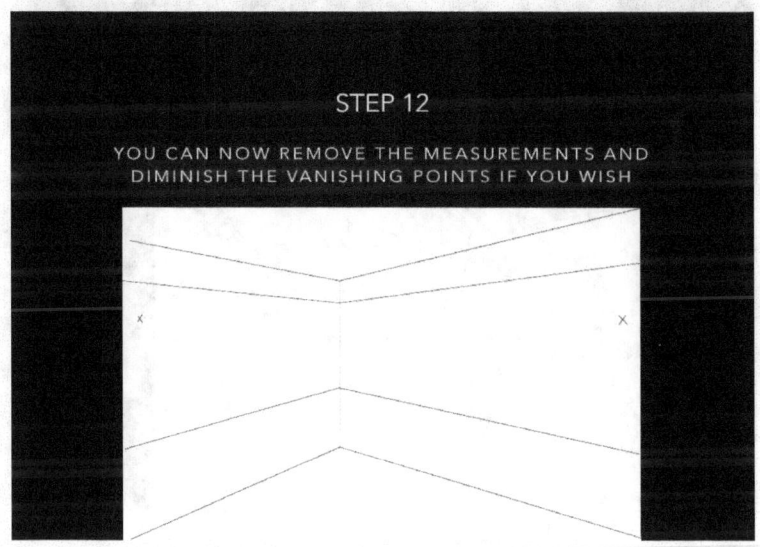

STEP 13

MARK THE UNITS OFF FOR THE MAJOR WALL USING
ONE OF YOUR RETURN WALL MEASUREMENT SYSTEMS

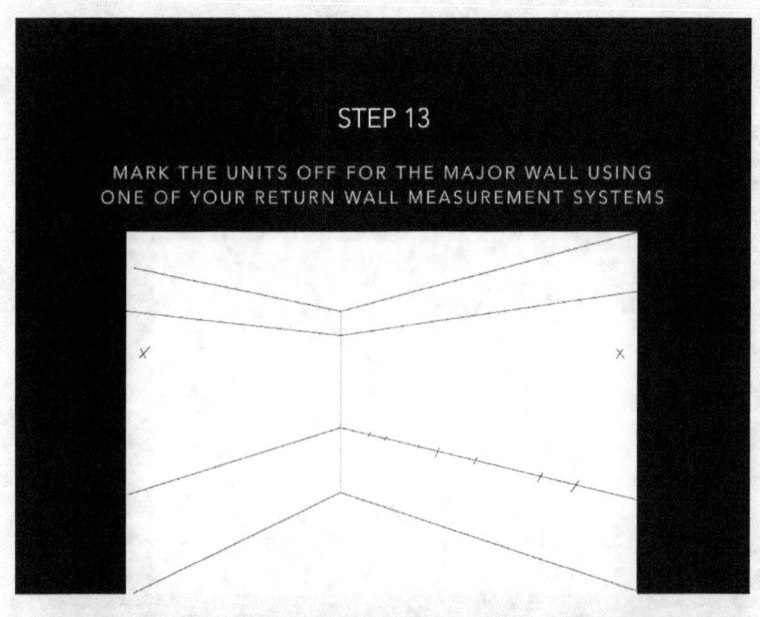

STEP 14

MEASURE THE DEPTH OF THE UNITS AND MARK THE
DIVISIONS ON THE FRONT OF THE RH CARCASSES

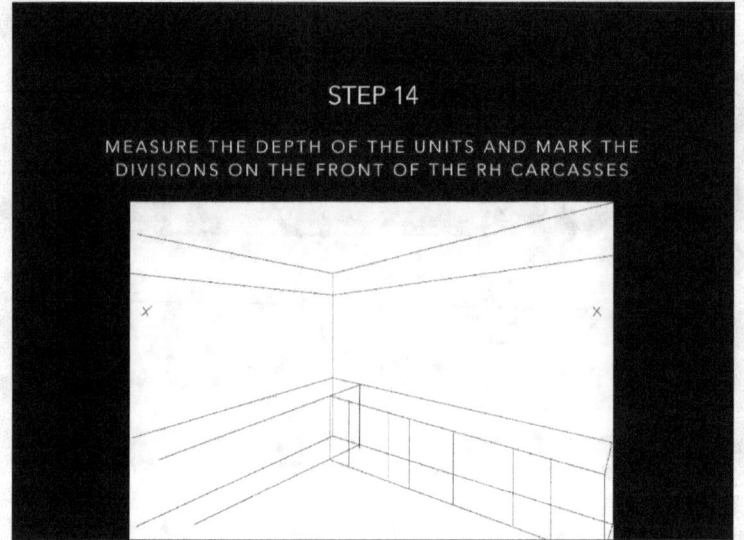

STEP 15

TIDY THE LINES- REMOVE THE HIDDEN LINES - MARK OFF
THE PLINTH & COMPLETE THE RH CARCASS OUTLINE

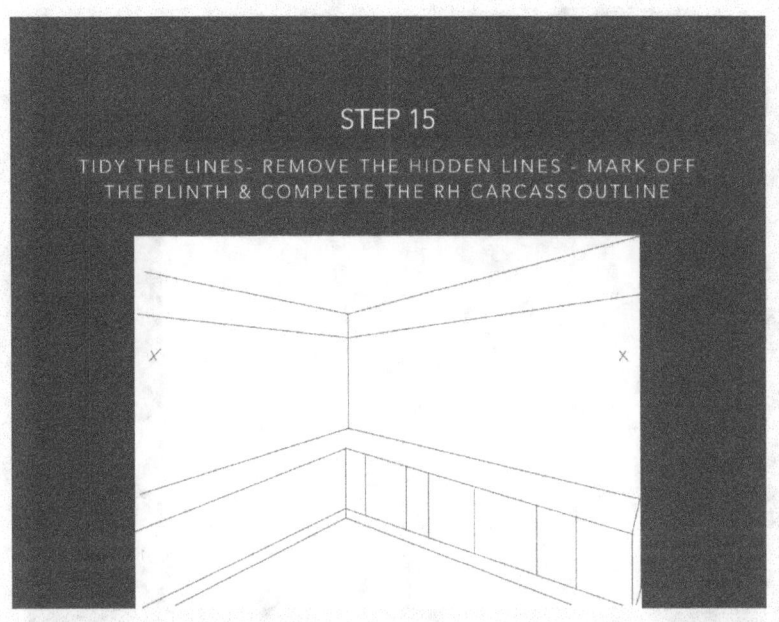

STEP 16

COMPLETE THE LH CARCASSING

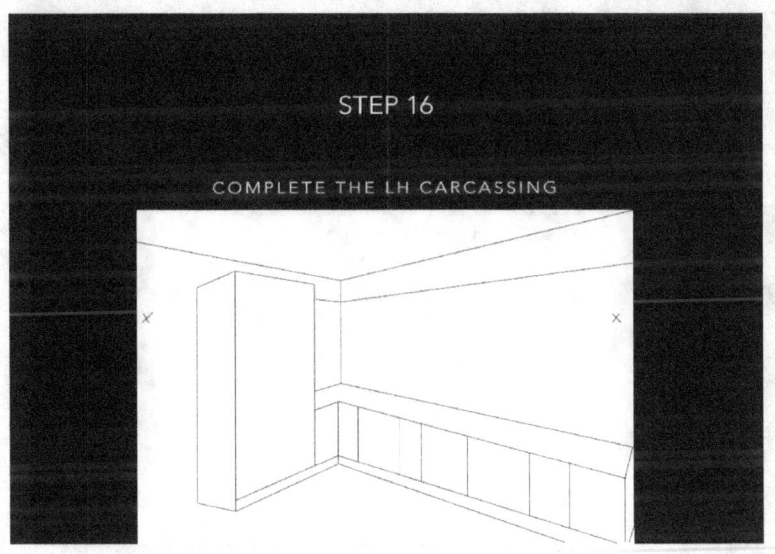

STEP 17

LOCATE THE WALL LINE

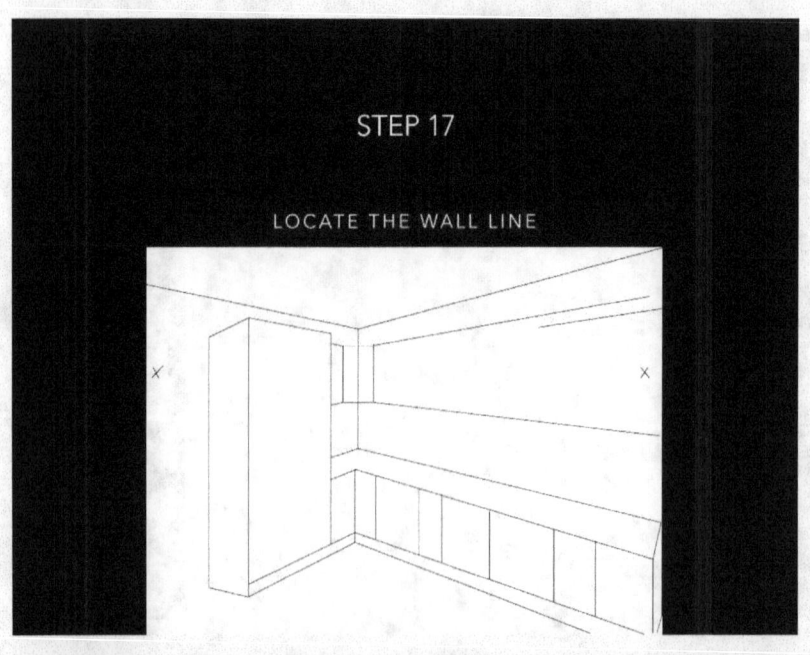

STEP 18

COMPLETE WALL CARCASSING

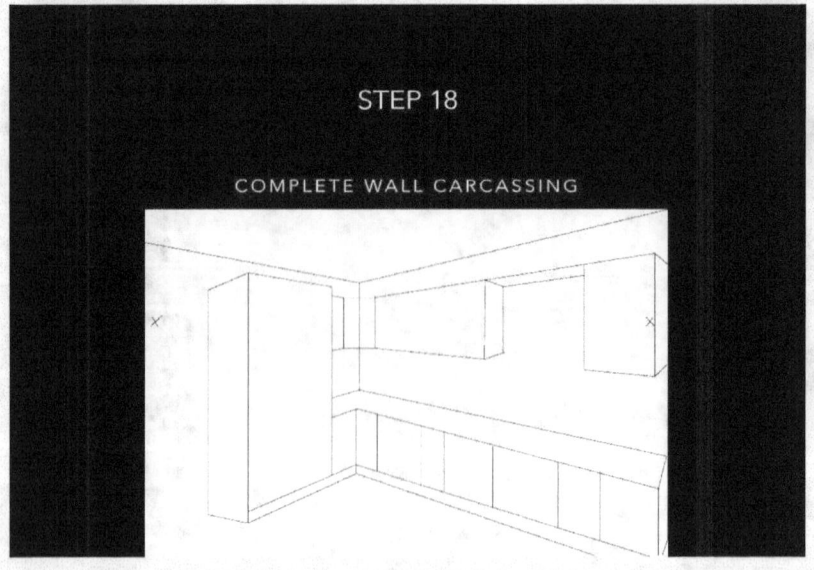

STEP 20

COMPLETE OTHER FEATURES AS PER CHOICE

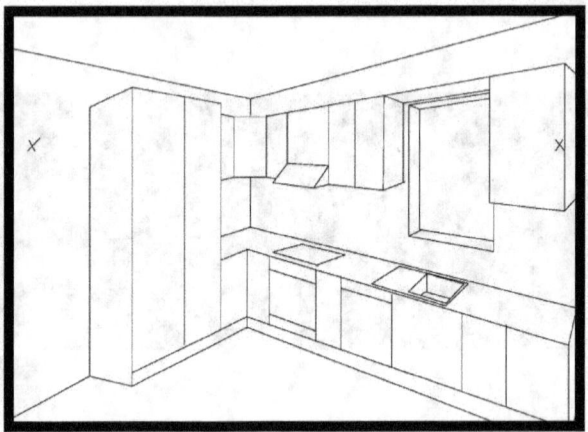

At this stage you can add cornice, light pelmet, worktop thickness, plinth inset etc. and proceed to final rendering.

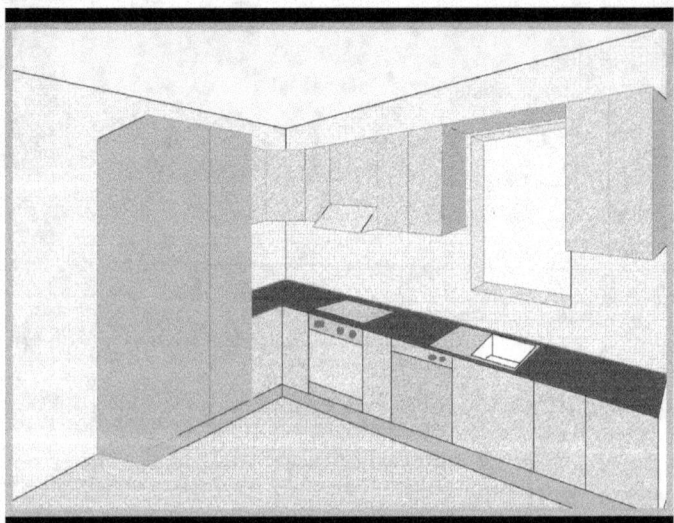

2 point Bathroom Method

Selecting geometric shapes makes the
bathroom presentation much simpler.

Use the modern geometric w.c. to match
the modern geometric showerbath and
complete that with furniture to match. You
can see in the illustration above the look
we are trying to create. We have chosen
the most geometric w.c. in our portfolio
and you can illustrate the choices with a
catalogue of examples.

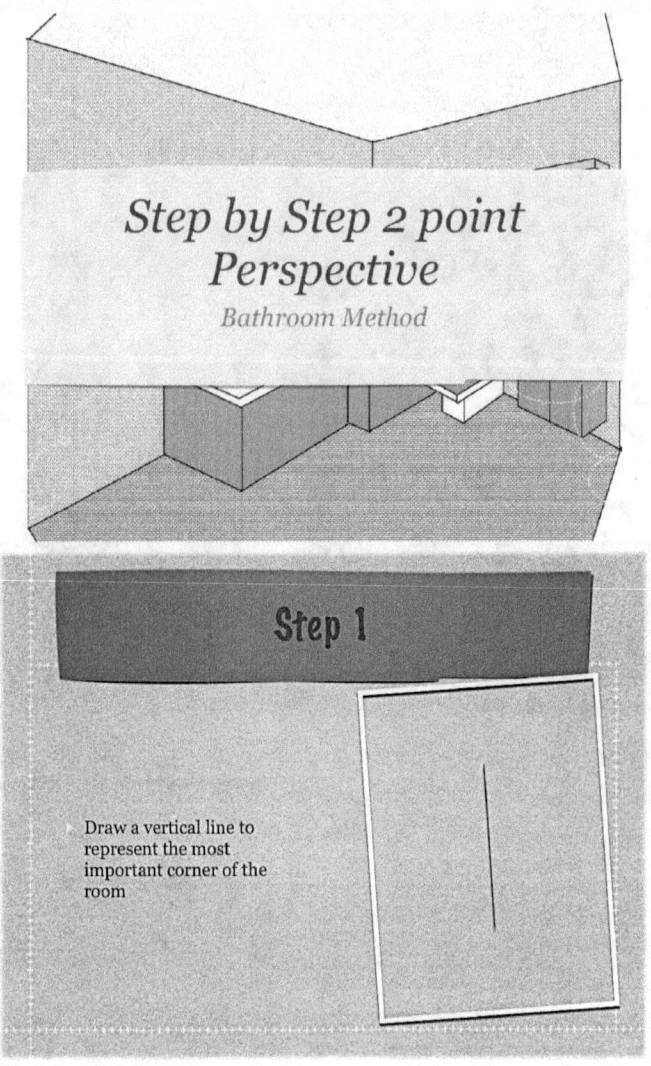

Step by Step 2 point Perspective

Bathroom Method

Step 1

Draw a vertical line to represent the most important corner of the room

Refer to the kitchen method to locate the horizon line and VP's and construct the wall.

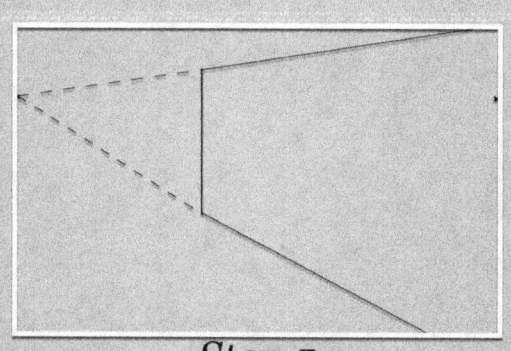

Step 5
Project the floor and ceiling.

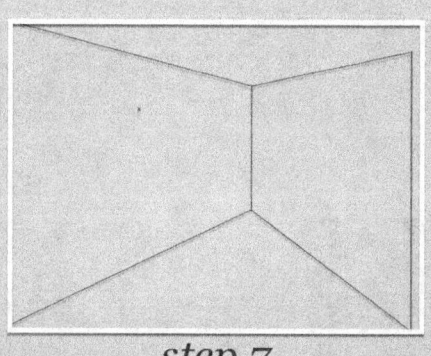

step 7
Measure the room and fix the end of the walls

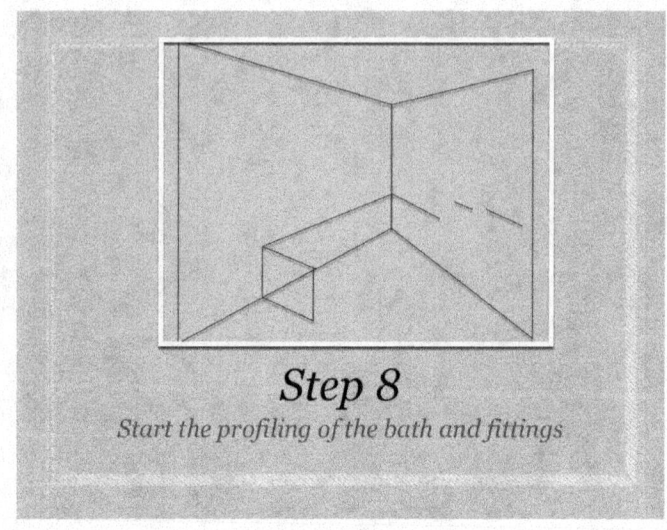

Step 8

Start the profiling of the bath and fittings

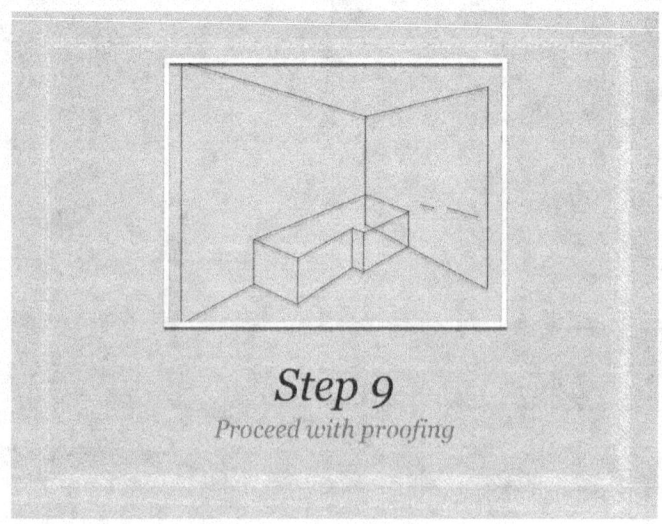

Step 9

Proceed with proofing

You can now remove some hidden lines

Step 11

Continue with basin unit profile - remember it is wall hung

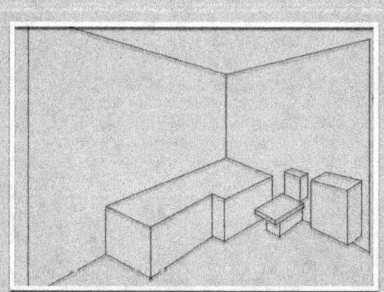

Step 12

Start building the toilet profile - - this is the most difficult part so we have used a geometric design following the bath style

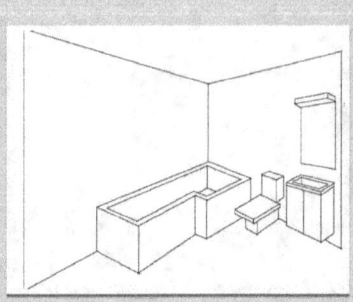

Step 14
Add detail as required

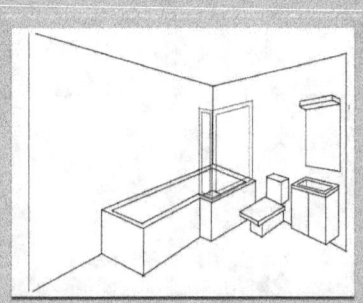

Step 15
Now add the bath shower screen - we are again using the ghosting method.

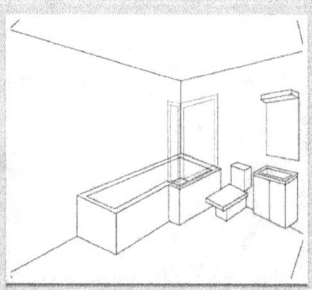

Step 16

Define the areas as required

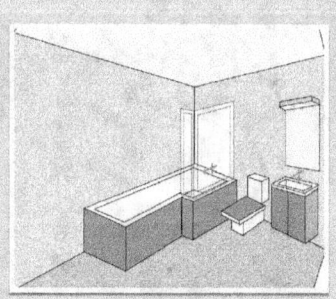

Step 16

Final view with rendering

5

Using a Computer

Almost everyone has a computer but not a drawing board in the 21st century.

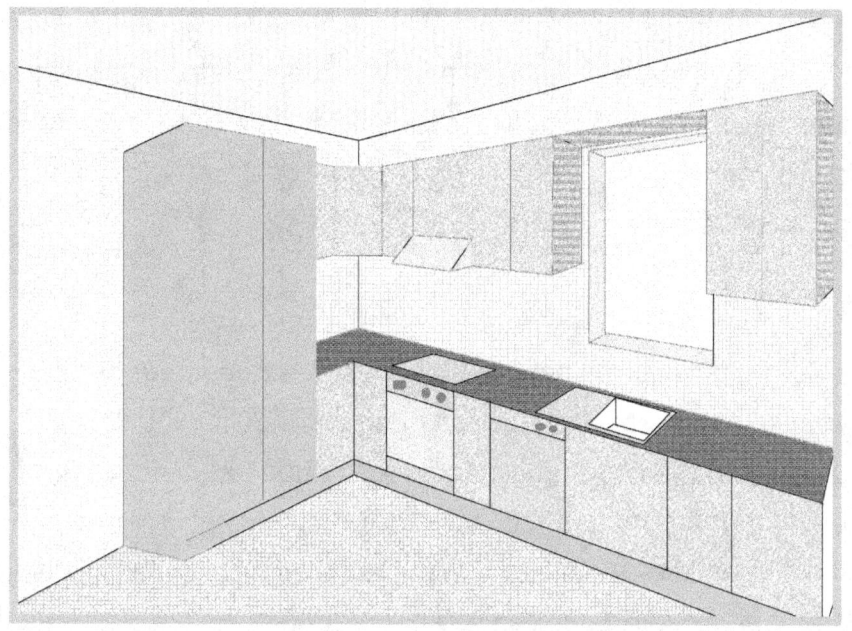

So if you would like to use the facilities on your computer - no problem. It is slightly trickier at first but with just a little practice the technique is easily developed. There are many FREE drawing programmes out there for both Mac and PC. Many of the programmes also have an angle restriction so you can set your angles. If not use a simple protractor at first and then you will be able to simulate the angles at will.

For the first few start of with pencil and paper drawing just to familiarise yourself with the technique and you can then move on to your computer programme probably after trialling just a couple of drawings

Most programmes have a simple 90° restriction for perfect vertical and horizontal lines so that part is built in. If your programme does not have angle restriction use a protractor for the first attempts and then you will gradually become used to the angles and be able to guestimate their positioning. Funnily enough when you get into real perspectives the lines are easier to draw on the computer as you have a vanishing point reference.

Thank you

Well I hope you have enjoyed this Mini Guide experience and perhaps you will join us again in another of these Guides. Please remember that the portrait guides are simpler and therefore cheaper than the landscape guides and the planning guides will vary because of the graphic content but the aim is always to produce an inexpensive and convenient guide.

TOTAL SUPPORT

If you need help go to our website at kbb2000.com and complete the contact form

Mini Guide Titles

other titles available but not all will be on general distribution

SURVEYING TECHNIQUES

EXTERIOR PRESENTATIONS

GRANNY FLATS

CLOAK ROOMS DRESSING ROOMS CLOSETS

KITCHEN WORKING TRIANGLE 2016

DOUBLE WORKING TRIANGLE

CREATIVE INTERIOR DESIGN USING A COMPUTER

CAD VS BRAIN

KITCHEN
PLANNING
ESSENTIALS

I POINT
PERSPECTIVE
& VANISHING
POINT

KITCHEN
PLANNING
APPLIANCES
ESSENTIALS

2 POINT
PERSPECTIVE
& VANISHING
POINT

KITCHEN
PLANING +
DESIGN

BIRDS EYE
PERSPECTIVE

BATHROOM
PLANNING

BEDROOM
PRESENTATION

BATHROOM
DESIGN

BATHROOM
PRESENTATION

www.ingramcontent.com/pod-product-compliance
Lightning Source LLC
Chambersburg PA
CBHW071245280526
45788CB00004B/1588